It Began with a Page

How Gyo Fujikawa
Drew the Way

Words by Kyo Maclear   Pictures by Julie Morstad

HARPER

An Imprint of HarperCollinsPublishers

It began with a page,
bright and beckoning.

It began with a mother writing a poem
and a father working a field and a little
girl named Gyo drawing a picture.

It was 1913, and Gyo was five years old.

That morning her mama said,
"*Ohayo*, sleepyhead!
It's going to be a busy day."

And it was.

Right until nightfall.

Mama's friends had come, and they were full of talk.

We sailed to America with our best kimono to see what we could be...

Such disappointment...
We need the vote.
we need rights.

Gyo held her rice bowl and
listened with curious ears.

Did Gyo know what she
wanted to be?

Not yet.

What she did know was that she liked to draw.
She loved the feel of the pencil in her hand. The dance and
glide of a line. How a new color could change everything:
a bright splash of yellow, a sleepy stroke of blue.

Every day she started

with an empty white page . . .

. . .and filled it with pictures.

At home, surrounded by drawing tools and books,
anything was possible.
But at school Gyo didn't feel that way.

At school, no one said, "That girl sure can draw."
No one noticed her colored pencils or box of paints.
No one even noticed when she moved away.

Gyo's new home was a fishing village near San Pedro,
California. A haven for Japanese Americans. A new life.
Roaming with her friends, Gyo felt weightless and free.

A ferry ride away, at her high school,
Gyo sometimes still felt invisible
among her mostly white classmates.

But her drawings caught the attention of two teachers.
Who was this girl whose eyes missed nothing, who could
sketch rivers and boats and birds like a dream?
Miss Cole and Miss Blum saw the energy in each line of
her drawings.

Gyo was too poor to
go to art school, but
Miss Cole found money
to pay her way.

Gyo was nervous to leave her home for the buzz and bustle of downtown Los Angeles. Not many girls, and even fewer Asian American girls, went to college in 1926.

But Gyo was determined.

She sketched statues, flowers, and faces. Her sketchbooks filled up, one after another.

Hungry to know more, Gyo set off for Japan, the land of her ancestors, to study traditional Japanese brush painting.

But the teachers were full of rules.

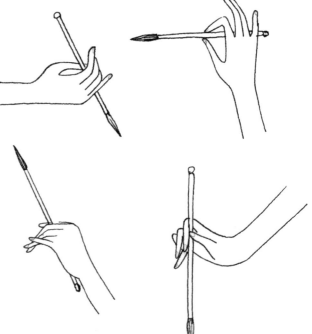

Instead, she traveled around the country doing her own learning:
wood blocks, carving tools, inks made of soot.

She lost herself in the prints of Hiroshige, Utamaro, and Hokusai . . .

. . . and floated in a beautiful sea of kimono.

Travel fed her dreams, but back in America it was time to earn money. For the next few years, Gyo worked long days, painting murals and drawing for magazines.

In 1941, she was offered a temporary job designing books at Walt Disney's studio in New York—a city filled with art and artists! It was hard for Gyo to leave her family, especially her mother.

Little did she know, things were about to get harder still.

In early 1942, terrible things were happening. Bombs and gunfire rocked the world. America was at war with Japan. Gyo was shocked to discover that anyone who looked Japanese or had a Japanese name was now suspected of being the enemy.

Japanese Americans living on the West Coast were ordered to leave their homes, their schools, their pets, their everything.

Gyo, along with others living on the East
Coast, was told to stay where she was.

On the West Coast, families preparing to
leave tried to sell their larger belongings,
like cars and furniture, to junk dealers.

But they were offered only pennies.
"I won't sell," said Gyo's mother, Yū.
Instead she set everything ablaze.

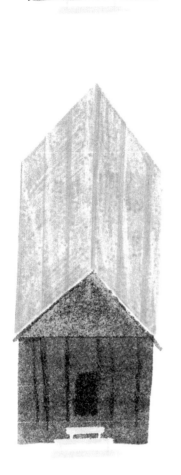

Gyo's family was sent to
a prison camp far, far away
from their home.

Gyo's heart was broken.

For the next three years the world shrank,
became tiny and terrible.

Now when she gazed at a white page,
no pictures would come.

Gyo mailed her family letters and sent gifts for
her new nephew, born in the camp.
But her heart would not mend.

Eventually, Gyo began to draw again.
She drew to keep her worries still and to save
money her family would need.

When angry strangers saw her as the enemy,
drawing comforted her.

When the world felt gray, color lifted her.
She wondered, could art comfort and lift others too?

When the war ended,
the Fujikawas were released.

With no house or
savings to call their own,
they had to start again.

For Gyo, the next fifteen years passed swiftly. There were stamps
to create, store windows to decorate, a children's book of poetry
to illustrate. There were two poodles who needed loving.

Now when Gyo walked around the city collecting ideas for her
pictures, she began to notice little changes around her.

Still, there was so much that hadn't changed.

At the library and bookshop, it was the same old stories—mothers in aprons and fathers with pipes and a world of only white children.

Gyo knew a book could hold more and do more. "A book," she told her poodles, "can be anything that anyone imagines it to be."

Gyo knew what she wanted to do. Every day she started with an empty page and filled it with pictures and words.

When her book was done she gave it to a publisher. . . . And what did they see?

Babies! Chubby-cheeked, squat-legged,
bouncy-bottomed babies. Naughty-nice,
oh-so-busy, toddle-crawling babies.

But the publisher said no.

No to mixing white babies and black babies.
It was not done in early 1960s America,
a country with laws that separated people
by skin color.

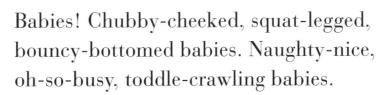

But Gyo would not budge.

She closed her eyes and remembered
all the times she had felt unseen and
unwelcome.

She looked the publisher in the eye and
said: "It shouldn't be that way. Not out
there in the streets. Not here on this
page. We need to break the rules."

Then she waited for them to
rethink their decision.
The babies waited too.
And waited.

But babies cannot wait.

Finally the publisher said yes.
And the book did well. Very well.
Babies loved it!

So Gyo kept going.

Welcoming kids in from the edges, from the corners,
from the shadows, Gyo let each child find a place.
Girls and boys freed from pink or blue, sharing
jokes, joys, mishaps, bruises.

All sprawling out across the bright page, ready for a
bigger, better world.

A timeline of Gyo's life

Gyo and Fred, 1920s

November 3, 1908:
Gyo Fujikawa is born in Berkeley, California, to first-generation Japanese American immigrants. Her mother, Yū, a poet and activist, and her father, Hikozo, earn a living as migrant farm workers (growing grapes).

July 4, 1910:
Gyo's only sibling, Yoshihiko Fred, is born. Fred will grow up to be a doctor (earning his way through medical school by working at a fruit stand).

Gyo with mother, Yū, and brother, Fred, 1913

1910s:
Gyo's mother takes in boarders and does embroidery to support the family. Her father continues farming and finds odd day jobs. It is hard to make ends meet. Hikozo is diagnosed with tuberculosis and slowly recovers.

Early 1920s:
Hoping to find an easier life, Gyo and her family move to Terminal Island, a small area of land between San Pedro and Long Beach, California. It's a lively fishing village of nearly three thousand Japanese American residents. Hikozo works in the tuna cannery. Fred and Gyo help out too when they can.

1922–1926:
Gyo attends San Pedro High School, where she throws herself into various art clubs. Her classmates know her as "Marguerite." Just before Gyo graduates, her teacher Helen Cole helps her get a scholarship to attend art college.

1926–1932:
Gyo studies at Chouinard Art Institute (now CalArts) in Los Angeles. In her free time she studies dance with modern-dance pioneer Michio Ito and befriends other Japanese American writers and artists.

1932:
Gyo spends a year traveling around Japan, where she develops a love of Japanese art and a stronger connection to her heritage.

1933–1937:
Gyo teaches night school at Chouinard Art Institute while juggling art jobs during the day. She works on several large murals and displays for department stores in Los Angeles and San Diego.

Painting a mural

1939:
Gyo joins Walt Disney Studios and begins promotional work on the movie *Fantasia* (1940).

May 1940:
Glamour magazine spotlights Gyo in an article titled "Girls at Work for Disney."

1941:
Gyo is sent to Disney's New York studios to work in the merchandising department. She leaves shortly after to work as an art director for a pharmaceutical company.

December 7, 1941:
Japan bombs US ships and planes at the Pearl Harbor military base in Hawaii. The United States declares war on Japan.

February 19, 1942:
President Franklin D. Roosevelt signs Executive Order 9066, clearing the way for Japanese Americans living on the West Coast to be sent to internment camps. Days later, Gyo's family and other Japanese Americans living on Terminal Island are ordered to leave their homes within forty-eight hours. Yū, Hikozo, and Fred are imprisoned at Santa Anita Park racetrack (where they live in horse stalls) and then sent to a prison camp in Jerome, Arkansas. Because Gyo is living on the East Coast, she avoids imprisonment. She visits her family and later describes Jerome as "a very bleak place . . . with barbed wire and a sentry walking around the wall with a bayonet."

Late 1940s–early 1950s:
Gyo works as a freelancer, doing commercial drawings, holiday cards, window designs, and magazine projects.

1957:
Grosset & Dunlap publishes a new edition of Robert Louis Stevenson's *A Child's Garden of Verses* featuring illustrations by Gyo. This leads to further book illustrations.

1963:
Gyo publishes *Babies*, the first book she writes and illustrates and one of the earliest children's books to use multiracial characters. *Babies* and its companion book, *Baby Animals*, quickly become bestsellers. Gyo decides to focus on writing and illustrating children's books from now on.

"I loved it, drawing children's books. I always wanted to do art work for children about children. It was just what I wanted to do."

In her New York studio apartment

"Although I have never had children of my own, and cannot say I had a particularly marvelous childhood, perhaps I can say I am still like a child myself. Part of me, I guess, never grew up."

1960s–1980s:
Gyo creates more than fifty books for children, including her favorites—and our favorites—*Oh, What a Busy Day!* (1976) and *Are You My Friend Today?* (1988).

1960s–1990s:
Gyo designs six United States postage stamps.

January 1973:
Gyo's father, Hikozo, dies at age eighty-nine.

December 1978:
Gyo's beloved mother, Yū, dies at age ninety-two.

November 26, 1998:
Gyo Fujikawa dies in New York City, three weeks after celebrating her ninetieth birthday.

A note from the author and illustrator

It began with a question: Who was Gyo Fujikawa?

We both loved Gyo's wonderful books but knew so little about their creator. We were full of questions. So we set out to find out more and to correct some of the muddled information circulating on the internet. Our search eventually led us to Gyo's family and her original papers in California. It's no exaggeration to say this book would not exist without the warmth and welcome of the Fujikawas—particularly Denson, Danny, Melissa, and Bonita—who shared family stories, photos, and archival materials.

So who was Gyo?

Gyo (pronounced "ghee-o") Fujikawa was an artist.

She made books, postage stamps, window art, murals, greeting cards, magazine covers—and built a celebrated career that spanned more than four decades in an industry that wasn't always welcoming to single women (not to mention those of Japanese American ancestry). During her time at Disney Studios, she worked alongside other Asian American and Mexican American artists who shaped the look of Disney films and books enjoyed all over the world.

Gyo was a trailblazer.

In her first author-illustrated book, *Babies*, she proposed showing "an international set of babies—little black babies, Asian babies, all kinds of babies." But this was the early 1960s, and a sales executive at Grosset & Dunlap told her that racial mixing would hurt sales in the American South. Gyo didn't care.

The book was published in 1963, a year before the Civil Rights Act made segregation illegal, and, along with its companion book, *Baby Animals*, went on to sell nearly two million copies in the United States alone. Not only did Gyo help break the color barrier in publishing, she also challenged old-fashioned ideas about what girls and boys could *do* or *be* or *feel*.

Gyo was a rule breaker.

Gyo inherited a passion for social justice and labor rights from her poet mother, Yū. For example, she would not work for publishers that didn't pay their artists a fair living wage. She was also one of the first children's book artists to ask for royalties. She encouraged other artists to do the same. "Let's not follow the old rules," she said. "Let's make new ones."

"Because I'm an artist myself, she continues to be an inspiration in my life. I am amazed to be related to such an amazing woman. To me she had such a subtle and graceful yet commanding presence—something I as a child could easily sense."
—Danny Fujikawa, songwriter and Gyo's great nephew

Gyo was an auntie and a dog lover.

Gyo always welcomed her niece and nephews and their children into her studio apartment in New York City. She enjoyed taking walks several times a day with her beloved poodles, Kiku and Suzu. In her later years, Gyo volunteered to deliver food to Japanese American seniors and former internees who were living alone in New York City. She continued to do school visits.

Gyo was a great bookmaker.

Along with her contemporaries Ellen Tarry and Ezra Jack Keats, Gyo made books that opened the door for today's conversations about diversity. She started with an empty white page and a wish for a bigger, better world and laid out a whole

dream—inviting publishers, teachers, readers, future writers, and illustrators to imagine a more inclusive future.

Not surprisingly, her books have been translated into seventeen languages and published in more than twenty-two countries.

Gyo Fujikawa's work has meant so much to us as artists and mothers. While we were both familiar with her books as children, we became more entranced with her sense of clarity, composition, and detailed delicacy as we worked on this book. Her depiction of children and sense of color continue to inspire us tremendously. We like to imagine ourselves playing follow-the-leader in a joyful and messy line, with Gyo somewhere near the front.

- Kyo and Julie

For Gyo Fujikawa, Miné Okubo, Ruth Asawa,
and all the nikkei women artists who led the way . . .
With great thanks to:
Julie, Jill, Tara, Jackie, Erin, and the Fujikawa family
—K.M.

For Gyo.
And to the babies, grandbabies,
and great-grandbabies of Rose and Tye Tasaka
—J.M.

Selected Bibliography

A Child's Garden of Verses, by Robert Louis Stevenson, 1957
Babies, 1963
Baby Animals, 1963
A Child's Book of Poems, 1969
A to Z Picture Book, 1974
Sleepy Time, 1975
Oh, What a Busy Day!, 1976
Come Follow Me, 1979
Are You My Friend Today?, 1988
Ten Little Babies, 1989

Sources

Hanawa, Yukiko. "The Several Worlds of Issei Women." Master's thesis, California State University at Long Beach, 1982.

Howard, John. *Concentration Camps on the Home Front.* Chicago: University of Chicago Press, 2008.

Matsumoto, Valerie. *City Girls: The Nisei Social World in Los Angeles, 1920–1950.* Oxford: Oxford University Press, 2016.

McDowell, Edwin. "Gyo Fujikawa, 90, Creator of Children's Books." *New York Times*, December 7, 1998.

Okihiro, Gary Y. *Encyclopedia of Japanese American Internment.* Santa Barbara, CA: Greenwood, 2013.

Wakida, Patricia. "Gyo Fujikawa." *Densho Encyclopedia* (online), accessed November 6, 2018.

Woo, Elaine. "Children's Author Dared to Depict Multiracial World." *Los Angeles Times*, December 13, 1998.

Wyman, Andrea. "Gyo Fujikawa, a Children's Illustrator Forging the Way." *Versed*, American Library Association, September–October 2005.

It Began with a Page: How Gyo Fujikawa Drew the Way
Text copyright © 2019 by Kyo Maclear
Illustrations copyright © 2019 by Julie Morstad
Photographs on pages 3, 45–47, and artwork on page 15 courtesy of the family of Gyo Fujikawa
All rights reserved. Manufactured in Spain by Estellaprint.
No part of this book may be used or reproduced in any manner whatsoever without written
permission except in the case of brief quotations embodied in critical articles and reviews.
For information address HarperCollins Children's Books, a division of HarperCollins
Publishers, 195 Broadway, New York, NY 10007.
www.harpercollinschildrens.com

Library of Congress Control Number: 2018964877
ISBN 978-0-06-244762-3

The artist used liquid watercolor, gouache, and pencil crayons
to create the illustrations for this book.
Typography by Erin Fitzsimmons
23 24   EP   10 9 8

❖

First Edition